COLORING AND ACTIVITY BOOK FOR TECH SUPPORT AND IT PROFESSIONALS

Published by E.B. Nesser (Beth Andresen)
Dallas, TX
December 2018

ISBN 13: 978-1731362537

ALL ABOUT ME: BRAG BOOK

MY NAME IS: _____

MY PROFESSIONAL SKILL SET: _____

_____

_____

MY MOST CREATIVE TECHNICAL ACHIEVEMENT: _____

_____

_____

_____

_____

I CAN GET LOST FOR HOURS WORKING ON: _____

_____

_____

_____

WORDS THAT DESCRIBE ME (CIRCLE ALL THAT APPLY):

IT Security	Nerd	Systems Admin	Programmer
Hipster	Technologist	Management	Always right
Developer	Old school	Attractive	Tech Support
Analyst	Networking	Star Wars fan	Architect

ALL ABOUT ME: BURN BOOK

MY SECRET NICKNAME IS: _____

I'M GROUCHIEST WHEN: _____

_____

THIS ONE TIME I REALLY SCREWED UP: _____

_____

_____

MOST ANNOYING CUSTOMER OR COWORKER: _____

_____

_____

_____

LEAST FAVORITE IT JOB EVER: _____

_____

_____

I AM GUILTY OF (CIRCLE ALL THAT APPLY)

Taking refreshments meant for clients   Cursing too much

Watching cat videos all day   Taking down the network

Cooking fish in the breakroom microwave   Hanging up on a customer

Lying about accidentally deleting a file   Clicking on a phishing link

"HOW I SPEND MY TIME" PIE CHART

What people think I do at work:

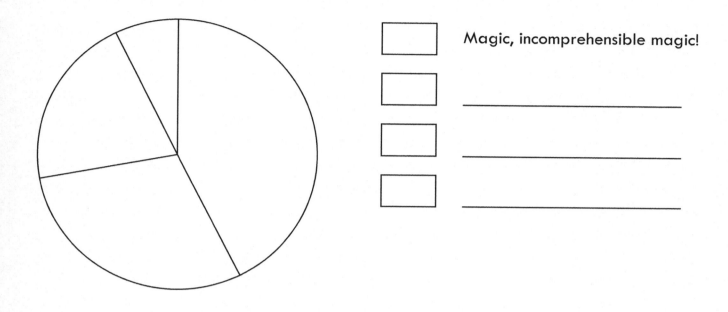

Magic, incomprehensible magic!

_____

_____

_____

What I really do at work:

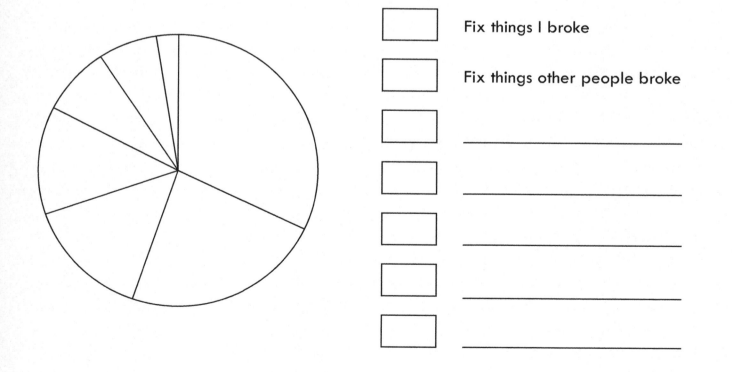

Fix things I broke

Fix things other people broke

_____

_____

_____

_____

_____

CIRCUIT BOARD MAZE

Fun fact: In 1903, German inventor Albert Hanson filed a patent for an insulating board made with layers of laminated flat foil conductors. While the first printed circuit boards officially appeared in consumer radios in 1936, the technology did not become widespread until after it had been tested, adapted and heavily used by the military during World War II.

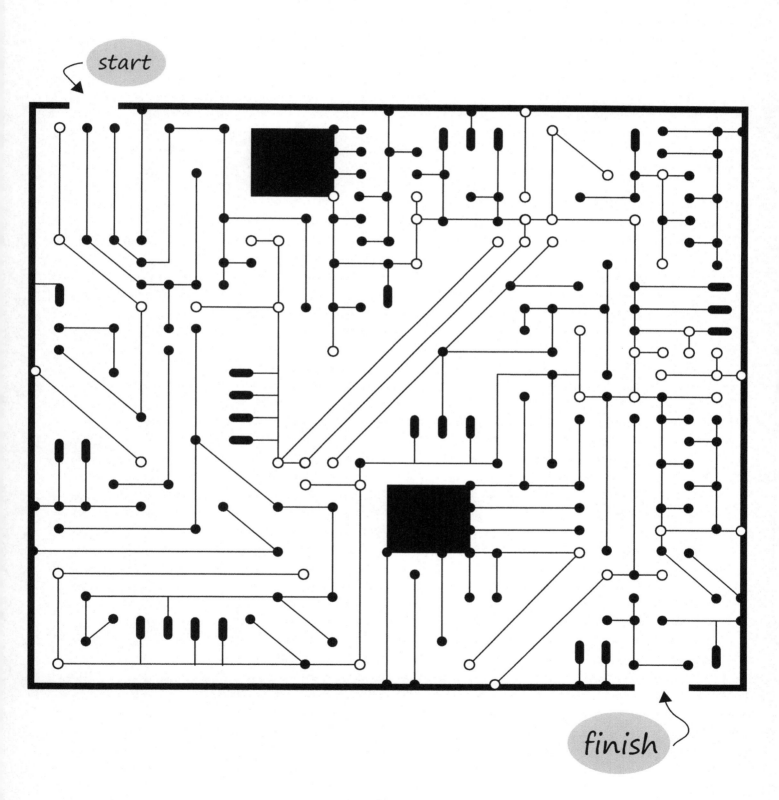

THE BROWSER CHALLENGE

1. Name each browser and the operating system for which it was originally developed.
2. Color in each browser icon accurately without peeking at anything digital.
3. Write the year each browser was introduced.

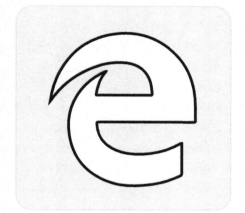

Browser: _____

Original OS: _____

Year introduced: _____

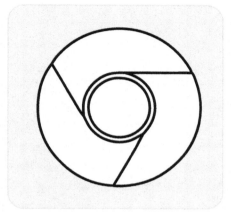

Browser: _____

Original OS: _____

Year introduced: _____

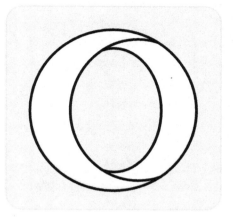

Browser: _____

Original OS: _____

Year introduced: _____

Browser: _____

Original OS: _____

Year introduced: _____

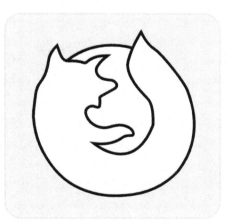

Browser: _____

Original OS: _____

Year introduced: _____

Browser: _____

Original OS: _____

Year introduced: _____

PEBKAC ERROR: COLORING PAGE 1.0

WORD SEARCH: PROJECT MANAGEMENT

Search up, down, forward, backward, and diagonally. Letters may be used more than once.

```
E T U B I R T S I D I M P L E M E N T E P I
E R E N O I T A C I N U M M O C A P L X R D
P F A E N I F E D I R E C T N E L M L P O E
O F D Y O H L A V O R P P A T A U A T E G N
C O N T I N U E T W C T R A N R T E E N R R
S K E T T T T R L I A U I A C R A A I S E A
A C G C I E A E N O S T M S G M K D S E S E
M I A M S I C T P S I M E E T I N G S K S L
A K E T N N E E A N I A G R N U L I E R S S
N N I I A G R Y I S S U E G F T M E T O E N
A N N C R A T E V A L U A T E A A Y U T S O
G G T A T I T I S V E R I F Y S L T N I O S
E M T I L E T N I O P K C E H C A L I N L S
R E O A G E P R O C U R E M E N T H M O C E
I N U D E V E L O P Y R S S E C O R P M N L
S Q U E Z I N A G R O U C O N D U C T I N G
K B E L B A R E V I L E D E X E C U T I O N
```

Agenda	Deliverable	Implement	Operations	Scope
Agile	Develop	Initiate	Organize	Scrum
Approval	Direct	Integrate	Phase	Tasks
Budget	Distribute	Issue	Plan	Team
Cancel	Documentation	Kick off	Process	Testing
Check point	Evaluate	Lessons learned	Progress	Time
Close	Execution	Manage	Procurement	Training
Communication	Expense	Meeting	Quality assurance	Transition
Conducting	Funding	Minutes	Resource	Verify
Continue	Gain	Monitor	Risk	Waterfall
Define				

SEARCHING FOR THAT PERFECT UNICORN

Laid-back startup searching for security analyst to build the next generation of data processing pipelines while discovering UX opportunities for digital marketing team. Candidates must be proficient in C#, HTML, and have experience teaching Office 365. Catered meals on Fridays!

Here is the applicant pool. One unicorn applied twice. Locate it by finding the identical pair.

INTERN EMPATHY

Mara is a Computer Science student interning at a software development company.
Draw an appropriate facial expression for each scenario, and describe what she is thinking.

An executive keeps asking Mara to get his coffee, and then leaves his empty trash cups on her desk to throw away.

_____

_____

Mara saves the day by writing a script that backs up a local file server right before an electrical storm hits and fries the server.

_____

_____

A coworker hazes Mara by sending her a zipped file containing a virus. She catches it in advance.

_____

_____

Mara's company offers her a full-time job upon graduation working as a technical writer, which is not her desired career path.

_____

_____

DECIPHERING VAGUE HELP TICKETS

Sometimes your customers submit incident reports that don't make any sense, like the one below. To figure out the real issue, circle every third letter. Ignore punctuation and spaces.

To: Tech support
Subject: Help me!

H(I), MY (D)ELETE LIKE SETUP ELUDES ME. MY BACKLOGS MAY POPULATE GENERIC HYPO-REWARDS. YOUR IMAGE GETS TIRING TO OBEY. ANY COOKIE?

What's the customer trying to say?

I D_____ __ _____.

___ __ _ ___ __ ____?

What's your response?

ACCESSORIZE A COWORKER

Eric is your new coworker. Fill in his other half using the grid, then accessorize appropriately based on Eric's role in your company. Suggestions below.

Consultant: Tie, clipboard, hopeful expression
Developer: Goatee, slogan on shirt, jeans
Designer: Ironic glasses, MacBook, sketchbook
Manager: Coffee mug, cell phone, org chart
Network Engineer: Cables, project plans
Sysadmin: Food stains (worked during lunch, again)
Tech Support: Headset, cart of broken printers
Training: Printed instructions, projector, door prizes

Eric's job title: _____

Accessories you added: _____

_____

_____

_____

Additional swag for Eric

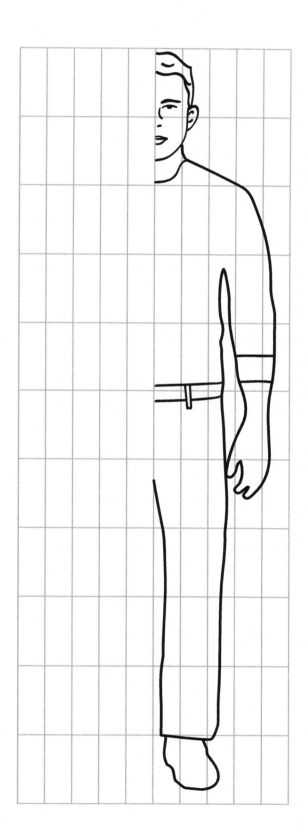

11

WHAT ARE THEY THINKING?

What are the Help Desk staff thinking when the new guy from marketing drops by with this request?

WHAT'S IN THE BOX?

You're assigned to clean out an old utility closet and find a mysterious box labeled TOP SECRET. Imagine what might be in the box for each scenario provided. Illustrate the contents if you like.

Dozens of a sought-after tech gadget from the 1980s or 90s.

What's in the box? _____

_____

Old VHS tapes from a higher-up's personal collection.

What's in the box? _____

_____

Printed files that could expose your workplace to a major lawsuit.

What's in the box? _____

_____

The geeky birthday present you've secretly been wanting for years.

What's in the box? _____

_____

SERVER ADMINISTRATION

You are deploying new servers today. Your boss, who likes beans *and* fart jokes, insists you name each server after a different legume (a bean or pea). How many can you name on your own?

You may add functional names to each server if you wish (web.chickpea; cluster1.chickpea, etc.)

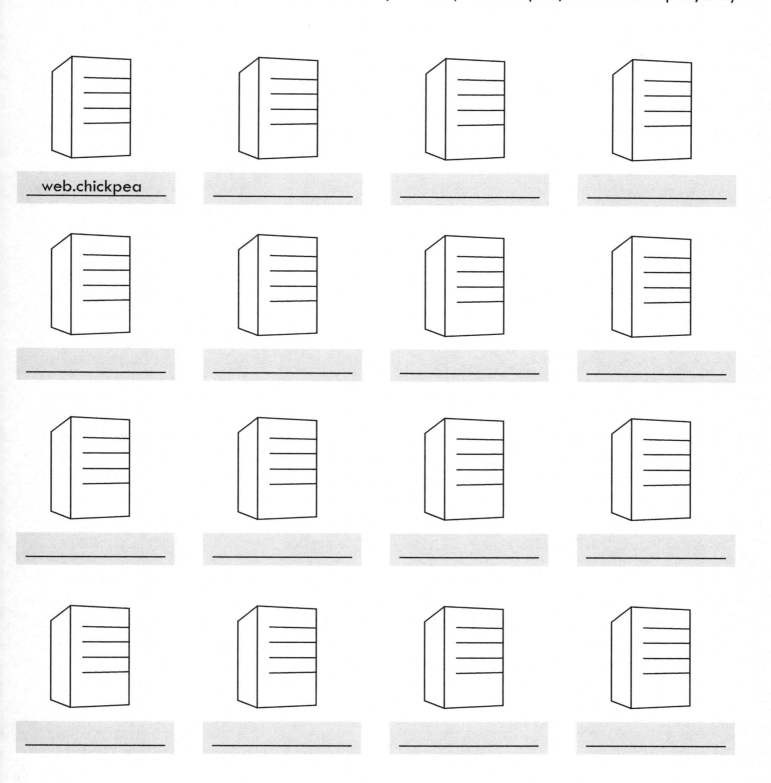

web.chickpea

"WE JUST HAVE A FEW CHANGES."

A shopping mall company hires you to create an app that provides directions to stores inside the mall. After months of client meetings, you create an innovative app... then this happens.

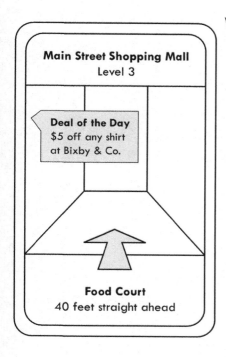

Main Street Shopping Mall
Level 3

Deal of the Day
$5 off any shirt
at Bixby & Co.

Food Court
40 feet straight ahead

THE APPLICATION YOU CREATED
GPS positioning
Robust SQL database
Browsable offline
Earn badges and deals for visiting stores
Advertising opportunities for storefronts
Data for over 50 worldwide locations

1000x hours development time

WHAT ACTUALLY LAUNCHES
A list of links to PDFs

Real Estate Holdings LLC
Store Maps

Click here to see a map of Main Street Shopping Mall in Tempe, AZ.

Click here to see a map of Main Street Shopping Mall in Denton, TX.

Click here to see a map of Main Street Shopping Mall in Buffalo, NY.

Click here to see a map of Main Street Shopping Mall in Baxter, MN.

Click here to see a map of Main Street Shopping Mall in Yukon, OK.

Rate our app!
☆ ☆ ☆ ☆ ☆

THE AWKWARD CLIENT MEETING

15

LUNCH-BREAK-AT-THE-CUBE-FARM MAZE

Rashid works at a cube farm and has exactly 30 minutes to eat lunch. Help Rashid make it from his cube to the lunch counter and back within this time frame... or Rashid will be fired.

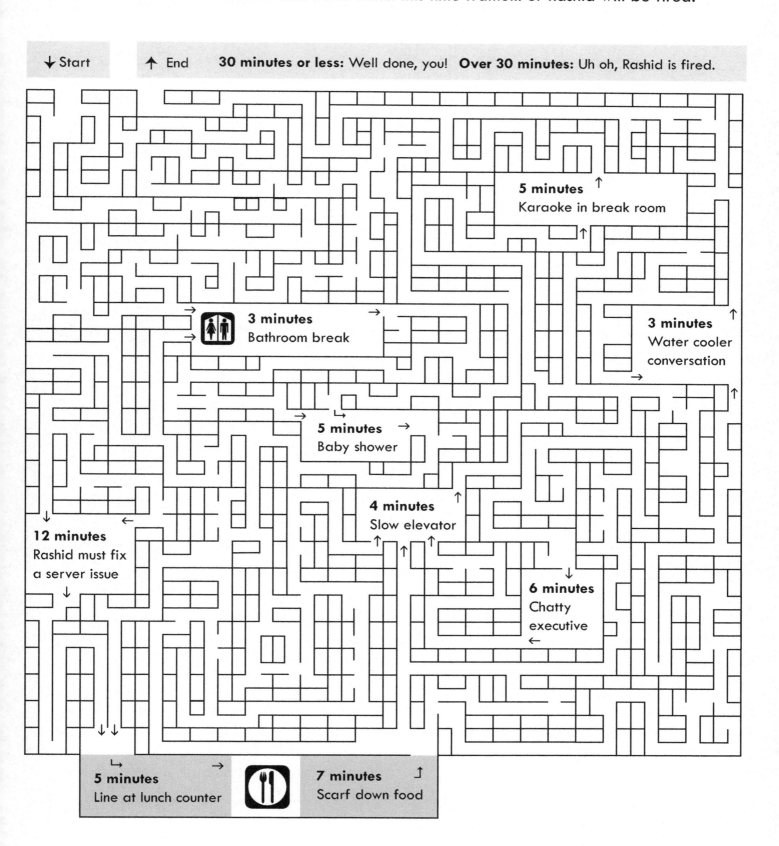

↓ Start   ↑ End   **30 minutes or less:** Well done, you!   **Over 30 minutes:** Uh oh, Rashid is fired.

5 minutes
Karaoke in break room

3 minutes
Water cooler
conversation

3 minutes
Bathroom break

5 minutes
Baby shower

4 minutes
Slow elevator

12 minutes
Rashid must fix
a server issue

6 minutes
Chatty
executive

5 minutes
Line at lunch counter

7 minutes
Scarf down food

A PUBLIC SERVICE ANNOUNCEMENT

Color in the letters with the ◆ symbol for a special message to the general public, brought to you from tech support workers everywhere.

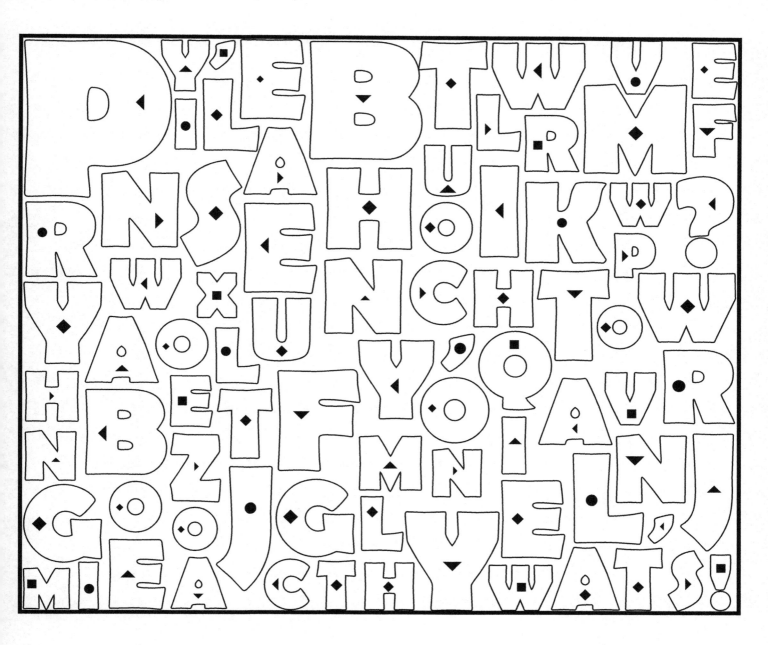

Spell out the secret phrase, reading from left to right, top to bottom:

_____

_____

17

RATE THE USER: SATISFACTION SURVEY

Your users have had a chance to rate you. Now, it's your chance to rate them. Have fun!

I know you *technically* only work on location, but could you drop by my house to help me with my printer? And help me get photos off my phone? Also, my FoxFire is running slow.

Your rating for this user: ☆ ☆ ☆ ☆ ☆

Additional comments: _____

What kind of name is Lisa? Are you even from this country? Let me talk to your manager.

Your rating for this user: ☆ ☆ ☆ ☆ ☆

Additional comments: _____

Don't talk down to me. I worked in tech support for 16 years. Just do what I'm asking and replace my router. Why do I have to keep telling you, it's leaking gigabytes.

Your rating for this user: ☆ ☆ ☆ ☆ ☆

Additional comments: _____

Well, my problems started after I emailed my password to this nice man I met online.

Your rating for this user: ☆ ☆ ☆ ☆ ☆

Additional comments: _____

CONFERENCE SWAG WORD SEARCH

The key to a great conference is a great program, but all that free swag doesn't hurt. How many free giveaways can you find in the puzzle below? Look for them by searching up, down, forward, backward, and diagonally.

```
S T E A M I C R O F I B E R C L O T H S E N N G I N R
T E D E C A L S G S L C V H O O N O T E B O O K C H E
I C O F F E E O A O R A S E S S A L G N U S T T C R T
C A I N S L W A B R S E S E S O L E G O S F T A A S P
K C F R I T O N T E A W T H T M I N G H M Y U N R N A
Y R L E A T T M N E I Y E S L S O H S P S A B N D I D
N E A L N O H G E O N K S B A I L U L D O L O P I A A
O D S L A B C Y M C O N M E C O G O S A U N I L G H R
T L H E O R A V R E N I B A R A C H O E N B S C A C E
E O D P E E E A E R L P P L O M R T H P Y R N N Y W
S H R O L T B M G C L S E A Y B P O S G L A A A E E O
E D I R E A F Q A K U C K A Z O O E S N E E D R E K P
R R V P C W C L S C A I L E W T V R T I D R I O D H R
E A E H T H T A O F O L N E H I E S N L H E A R D A A
C C T T R E L E R G E R R S N F A E I L E B D E D B F
H S H I O F E U L R A C P K C R D T M E A Y D N E D A
W S I W N I S E B L H E K O H I I A H C D I E N R P N
R E S E I T S M E A A A O S G S N L T N L L O A O K N
I N B I C B U T R K E W P L A B N O A A A B D L H C Y
S I O N F I D G E T S P I N N E R C E C M A O P C A P
T S O A A T E R S I M M U G A E S O R E P S R Y T P A
B U K E N R S T A P P L E W A T C H B S H B A A A K C
A B E B H O W S S E P I W N E E R C S I O S N D T C K
N W I N D S H O R T S T A M A G O Y R O T O T E B A G
D B S O O T T A T Y R A R O P M E T O N P E A R Y B N
```

Items you found:

_____

_____

_____

_____

_____

_____

_____

_____

_____

_____

_____

_____

_____

_____

_____

_____

_____

_____

_____

_____

_____

_____

_____

Reward yourself: How many items did you find?

Under 20:   Help yourself to a free highlighter.
21 - 30:   Grab a highlighter and a tote bag.
31 - 40:   Grab a highlighter, tote bag, and a travel size stain remover
41 - 50:   Grab all of the above, plus a luggage tag
51+   Grab all of the above, plus ultimate bragging rights

Which swag do you like the best? _____

Which one is the nerdiest? _____

GIFTS FOR IT PROFESSIONALS

So you work in IT, which means when it's the gift giving season, people may be mystified about what to give you (other than this coloring book). Pick a recipient for each nerdy gift listed below and imagine the person's reaction.

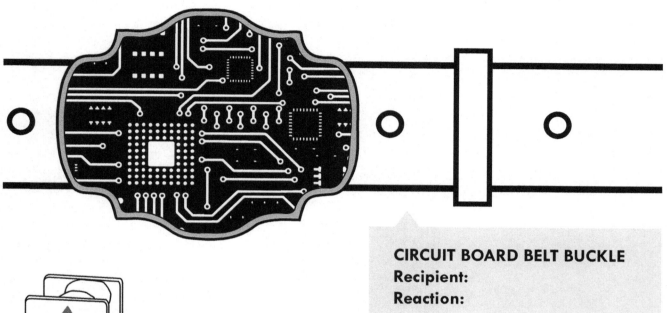

CIRCUIT BOARD BELT BUCKLE
Recipient:
Reaction:

USB FLASH DRIVE CUFF LINKS
Recipient:
Reaction:

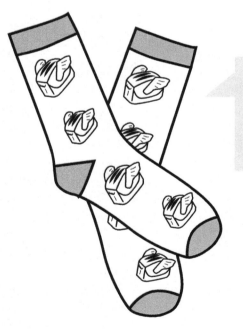

SOCKS WITH FLYING TOASTERS
Recipient:
Reaction:

VINTAGE iMAC G3 AQUARIUM
Recipient:
Reaction:

MEETING BINGO

Next time you're stuck in a long meeting, make it more interesting by playing BINGO. You are encouraged to shout out BINGO if you win.

By the way, BINGO stands for *But It's Never Getting Over!*

B	I	N	G	O
A manager tells a bad joke. People fake laugh.	Bottled water	Two or more people wearing yellow	Somebody continuously interrupts others	Design or development team is bashed
The word "network"	More meetings are scheduled	Somebody burps	Performance reviews mentioned	Somebody secretly watches YouTube videos
At least one polo shirt	Time tracking	FREE	The word "DevOps"	Over 25% of attendees wear eyeglasses
Questions, so many questions...	Somebody forgets to silence their phone	The word "deadline"	Two or more people show up late	Somebody is dreadfully underdressed
The phrase "scope creep"	Customer service	Project Management	Food is discussed	Somebody takes credit for your great idea

DO THE MATH

Decipher the secret code below by 1) solving the math problem and 2) translating the answer to a letter using the code.

$\frac{125}{5}$ 3×5 3×7 3×6 $\sqrt{-1}$ $(-1)^2$ $\frac{42}{14}$ $\frac{5.5}{.5}$ $\frac{42}{2}$ 2^4 3^2 $\frac{57}{3}$

$\frac{105}{7}$ 2×7 $\frac{6\times6}{3}$ $\frac{20\times5}{4}$ $\frac{2^2}{4}$ $\frac{38}{2}$ $\frac{49}{7}$ 5×3 $\frac{60}{4}$ $\frac{76}{19}$

$\frac{5\times4}{10\times2}$ $\frac{76}{4}$ 5^2 $\frac{75}{5}$ 7×3 $\frac{6^2}{2}$ 2×9 $\frac{5^2}{5}$ $\frac{95}{5}$ $\frac{80}{2^2}$ $\frac{30}{2}$ $\frac{36}{2}$ $\frac{30}{6}$.

TRANSLATION GUIDE

A	B	C	D	E	G	I	K	L	N	O	P	R	S	T	U	Y
1	i	3	4	5	7	9	11	12	14	15	16	18	19	20	21	25

NAME THE PORTS

Some of the ports below date back more than fifty years. How many can you name?
If you'd like a clue, flip the page to see a list of potential ports.

Note: The ports are not drawn to scale.

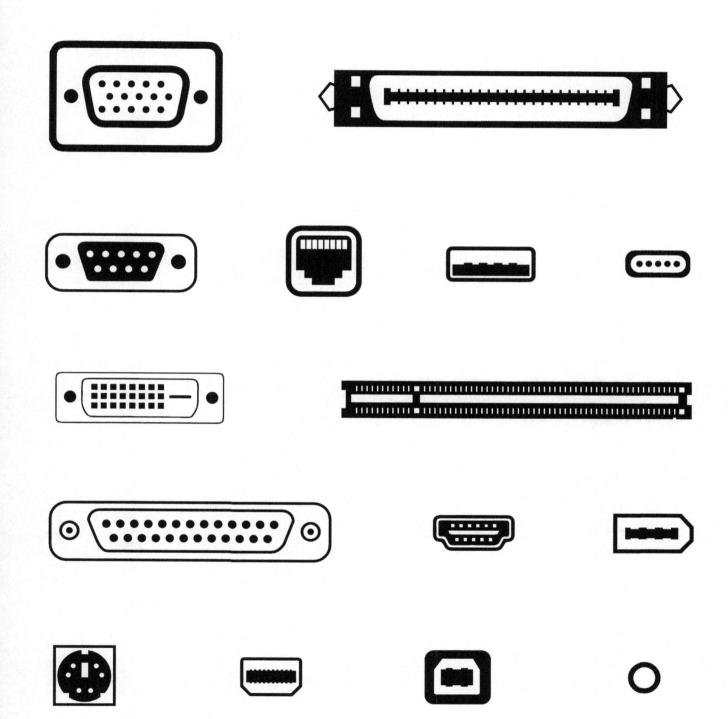

Secret hint: these ports are shown on page 24.

Audio In
Conventional PCI
DVI-D Dual Link
Ethernet
Firewire 400
HDMI
MagSafe 2 (Thunderbolt)
Mini DisplayPort
Parallel
PS/2
SCSI 1
Serial
USB A
USB B
VGA

SPOT THE DIFFERENCES: BUGS IN THE CODE

LOST AND FOUND

How many USB cables are in your lost and found drawer? Notice that some cables are complete (plugs on both ends) while others are incomplete (only one cable per end.) How many of each type are in the drawer?

Complete cables: _____   Broken cables: _____

CALL CENTER MAZE

You're working the phones today. Can you safely make it from 9 to 5?

Start - 9 a.m.

People think if they yell at you, you'll fix things faster. Weird, right?

Your manager listens in the first time you ever hang up on somebody

No lunch break, stuck on a call with a rambling high-priority customer

You drool on your headset & it disintegrates

Two hours to track down a non-existent serial number that the user mistyped

The person next to you had raw onions for lunch and keeps yawning

End - 5 p.m.

PEBKAC ERROR: COLORING PAGE 3.0

IT ACRONYMS AND INITIALISMS

How many of the acronyms and initialisms below can you name without consulting the www?

ASNI _____

API _____

CAT _____

CPU _____

CRT _____

CSS _____

DCE _____

DHCP _____

DSL _____

EOL _____

FTP _____

HTTPS _____

ISP _____

LAN _____

Mbps _____

MDF _____

POP _____

RAM _____

SSH _____

TCP/IP _____

USB _____

W3C _____

5 or fewer:	Well, there's alwyas Google.
6 - 10:	Not bad.
11 - 15:	Very respectable.
16 - 20:	Well done!
21+:	Flip to page 8. That's you!!!

APRIL FOOL'S DAY: SAILOR FLOP DAY

As an April Fool's Day joke, somebody has gone through your building and replaced the signage with anagrams. How many signs can you unscramble?

Singular words may be scrambled into multiple words. Example: Sea Duty = Tuesday

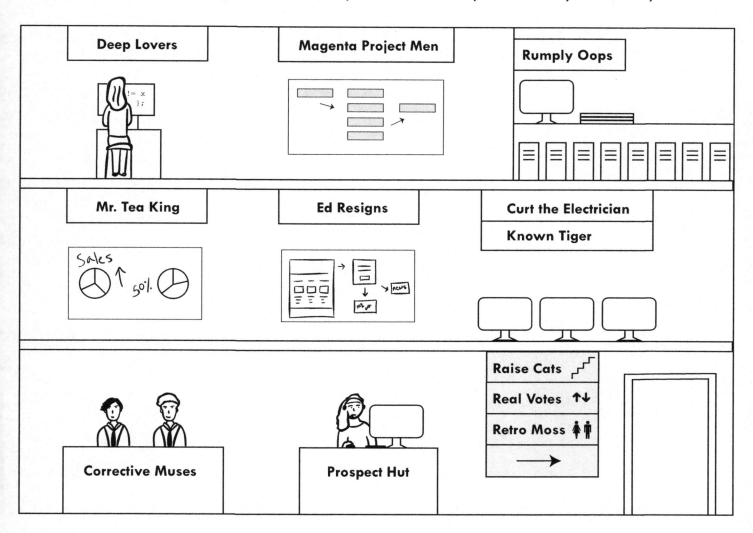

Bonus activity: Unscramble the bolded words in this memo from the higher-ups.

```
ATTENTION ALL MEAT MEATS:

Drop by the barker moo for cookies and cake as we congratulate
those receiving room points. We look forward to starting the
next a scary life together, working as meat meats.

Happy salary dip fool,
The Cutie Vexes
```

30

BUZZ WORD BUZZ KILL: WORD SEARCH

Take it to the next level: see how many of these top-notch words and phrases you can find by utilizing your core competencies. Search up, down, forward, backward, and diagonally. At the end of the day, if you find all the words, you'll know this is your omnichannel wheelhouse.

```
G L U I L T H O U G H T L E A D E R E Z I L I T U X T Y P
T I U R F G N I G N A H W O L T E A W H E E L H O U S E T
P F C T F I H S M G I D A R A P A X T E M O C T A R T S V
A E R I E K E N N N W O D L L I R D S L E V E R A G E A T
Y H E D M D E P O T T Y P G E R I E A I S D B I R D L S U
M A F O P G I V E N D E A T R W A M T T L O M L R N A I R
S C A L A B L E I E H M Y W D C M G I A C O E H A E C O N
L K C O T H E O N T E M O N U S T N T U N V T N I N I N K
G S N R H E P W O C U R A T E D S I A T E N I Y U B T S E
C A I N Y E D T H I A B T N E D G P A L U T N E P R R O Y
C B F I C R P A R N S I T L A I M E T P T U O H C A E R S
E O D I A U N E I G N I P D G L X A N T S I N P A V T O
V F R I P G N S A G D V A T T H E E N D O F T H E D A Y L
I P N E E C K E E P E S A O O N P U Y P A N C T N K S O U
T E T R C C C D T R E T T O R E W O P M E E A I E F W N T
A S L O U O G U A I P A A W O R D R M U P N R H X E O U I
N R E D D E M B R E D R D R A W R O F G N I O G T Z L S O
L E C H O W L P N A I T K R E S V B M E A L O F G I F E N
A C O F G E O G E D V R R A B I D U D E D F O R E G K R F
T N S L G I A T N T E E A N N P R S L E D F A T N R R S E
I E Y O Y G E I S H E K D G O A T T R O G O G R E E O T E
G U S W E S M O N E Y N P O N I E S T M A E R T S N W O D
I L T M L E T S U N P A C K T H I S Y A Y K I T E Y D R T
D F E E V E R Y O U R T H I N K I N G O T A B I B S O Y A
S N M I J O K E S T O I N T E R N E T O F T H I N G S L C
T I H O W D O E S T H I S N O S N O S S G N I N R A E L O
```

Action item
At the end of the day
Bandwidth
Buy-in
Core competencies
Curated
Cutting edge
Dark data
Deep dive
Deliverable
Digital detox
Digital native
Downstream
Drill down

Ducks in a row
Ecosystem
Empathy
Empower
Engagement
Game changer
Going forward
Hive mind
Influencer
Internet of things
Learnings
Let's unpack this
Leverage
Life hacks

Low hanging fruit
Manage up
Moving parts
Next level
NextGen
Our thinking
Paradigm shift
Ping me
Price point
Punt
Reach out
Robust
Scalable
Silo

Stakeholder
Step up to the plate
Stratcom
Synergize
Take offline
Thought leader
Tribe
Turnkey solution
User story
Utilize
Vertical
Wheelhouse
Workflow

CUSTOMER APPRECIATION BADGES

Show your appreciation for your customers with a quick note.

WHO'S AWESOME? YOU'RE AWESOME!

☐ Solved your own problem.
☐ Provided the details I needed.
☐ Said thank you.
☐ Googled it yourself.

☐ Exhibited patience.
☐ Left genuine, positive feedback.
☐ _____
☐ _____

Presented to _____   Date: _____

CLEAR COMMUNICATOR AWARD

You make my life easier!

Awarded to: _____

For: _____

FIRST RESPONDER AWARD

Thank you for reporting a problem before it became an emergency.

Awarded to: _____

Day and time: _____

HOORAY FOR OWNING YOUR MISTAKE!

To err is human.
To admit it to tech support is divine.

Awarded to: _____

For: _____

GREAT SENSE OF HUMOR

You brightened my day...
I haven't laughed so loud in ages!

Awarded to: _____

For: _____

WHO'S AWESOME? YOU'RE AWESOME!

☐ Solved your own problem.
☐ Provided the details I needed.
☐ Said thank you.
☐ Googled it yourself.

☐ Exhibited patience.
☐ Left genuine, positive feedback.
☐ _____
☐ _____

Presented to _____   Date: _____

CUSTOMER HALL OF SHAME

Need to vent? We suggest only giving out these awards if you want a visit with HR.

WAIT, YOU EXPECT ME TO BE CHEERFUL AFTER YOU:

- ☐ Invoked my manager.
- ☐ Insulted my knowledge.
- ☐ Insinuated I was worthless.
- ☐ Interrupted me repeatedly.
- ☐ Disregarded my instructions.
- ☐ Declared yourself the expert.
- ☐ Blamed me for your problem.
- ☐ _____

Presented to _____ Date: _____

Reason: _____

NO THIS IS NOT AN EMERGENCY.

Presented to _____

Reason: _____

_____

SAME CUSTOMER, SAME QUESTION...

Presented to _____

Reason: _____

_____

NO I CAN'T FIX YOUR PERSONAL GEAR.

Presented to _____

Reason: _____

_____

HA HA! IT ACTUALLY WAS UNPLUGGED!

Presented to _____

Reason: _____

_____

WAIT, YOU EXPECT ME TO BE CHEERFUL AFTER YOU:

- ☐ Invoked my manager.
- ☐ Insulted my knowledge.
- ☐ Insinuated I was worthless.
- ☐ Interrupted me repeatedly.
- ☐ Disregarded my instructions.
- ☐ Declared yourself the expert.
- ☐ Blamed me for your problem.
- ☐ _____

Presented to _____ Date: _____

Reason: _____

COWORKERS FOR THE WIN

Good colleagues are worth their weight in gold. Share your appreciation here.

WELL DONE! I APPRECIATE THE WAY YOU:

- ☐ Troubleshoot.
- ☐ Keep it together under pressure.
- ☐ Create great documentation.
- ☐ Write code.
- ☐ Collaborate with colleagues.
- ☐ Handle difficult customers.
- ☐ Take charge.
- ☐ _____

Presented to _____ Date: _____

IT SUPERHERO!

All around greatness!

Awarded to: _____

For: _____

CREATIVE SOLUTION

It's elegant. It's innovative. And it's effective. Way to go!

Awarded to: _____

For: _____

EMBARRASSING (BUT FUNNY) TYPO.

High five – once we're all done laughing at you.

Awarded to: _____

For: _____

SPECTACULAR APPEARANCE

Stunning haircut. Sparkling hygiene.

Awarded to: _____

For: _____

WELL DONE! I APPRECIATE THE WAY YOU:

- ☐ Troubleshoot.
- ☐ Keep it together under pressure.
- ☐ Create great documentation.
- ☐ Write code.
- ☐ Collaborate with colleagues.
- ☐ Handle difficult customers.
- ☐ Take charge.
- ☐ _____

Presented to _____ Date: _____

PEBKAC ERROR: COLORING PAGE 4.0

SOLUTIONS

5: THE BROWSER CHALLENGE

The question about browser release date is tricky, since many browsers had beta launches followed by official public releases and quickly evolved during this short time period.

Microsoft Edge, released in 2015 for Windows 10 and Windows 10 mobile as a replacement for Internet Explorer.

Chrome, released in 2008 for Microsoft Windows.

Opera, developed in 1994 and publicly released in 1996 as shareware for Microsoft Windows. Other operating systems, including Apple Macintosh, QNX and BeOS were soon included.

Safari, released in 2003 for Mac OS X.

Mozilla Firefox, developed in 2002; released in 2004. Early releases ran on Microsoft Windows, Mac OS X, and Linux systems.

Netscape Navigator, beta versions released in 1994-1995. The groundbreaking browser was popular and ran on multiple operating systems, including Windows, Macintosh, OS/2, Unix, and Linux. Fun fact: JavaScript was created specifically for Netscape.

Netscape's history is fascinating; if you'd like a holistic look at how early browsers were interconnected, you may enjoy reading about how Netscape came to be and how it passed out of existence.

7: PROJECT MANAGEMENT WORD SEARCH

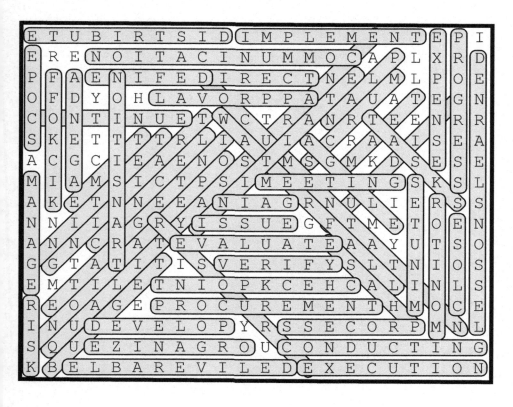

SOLUTIONS (CONTINUED)

8: SEARCHING FOR THAT PERFECT UNICORN

Note the placement of the eye sparkle, eyelashes, forelock, mane, and the direction of the horn twirls.

9: INTERN EMPATHY

Author's note: the situation with the empty trash cups actually happened, though not to me.

10: DECIPHERING VAGUE HELP TICKETS

Secret message:
I deleted my computer. How do I get it back?

14: SERVER ADMINISTRATION

This boss is based on a real person. Aren: you know who you are, and you know what you did.

17: A PUBLIC SERVICE ANNOUNCEMENT

Secret Message: Let me show you how to Google that.

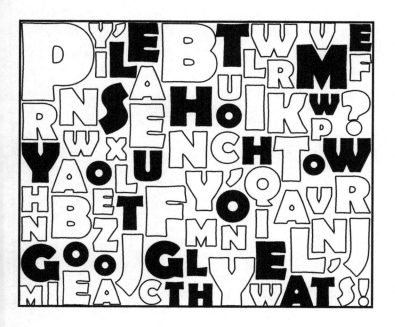

SOLUTIONS (CONTINUED)

20: CONFERENCE SWAG WORD SEARCH

The following items were hidden in the word search. You may have found others.

Apple Watch
Backpack
Beach Towel
Beanie with Propeller
Bluetooth Speakers
Breath Mints
Business Card Holder
Button
Calendar
Candy
Carabiner
Cardigan
Chocolates
Coasters
Coffee
Day Planner
Decals
Deodorant
Ear Buds
Electronic Fan
Fanny Pack
Fidget Spinner
FitBit
Flash Drive
Flashlight
Flask
Frisbee
Garment Bag
Go Pro Camera
Golf Tees
Kazoo

Keychain
Lanyard
LED Headlamp
Legos
Microfiber Cloth
Mouse Pad
Mug
Noise-Canceling Headphones
Notebook
Pencils
Polo Shirt
Power Adapter
Power Charger
Screen Wipes
Slinky
Steak Knives
Sticky Notes
Sunglasses
Surface Pro
Temporary Tattoos
This Book
Tote Bag
Umbrella
Vase
Wallet
Water Bottle
Webcam
Wind Shorts
Wristband
Yoga Mat

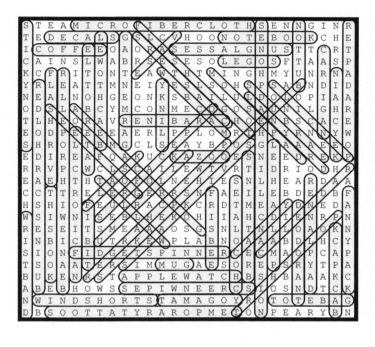

24: NAME THE PORTS

VGA

SCSI 1

Serial

Ethernet

USB A

MagSafe 2
Thunderbolt

DVI-D Dual Link

Conventional PCI

Parallel

HDMI

Firewire 400

PS/2

Mini DisplayPort

USB B

Audio In

SOLUTIONS (CONTINUED)

26: LOST AND FOUND

18 complete cables
5 broken cables

29: IT INITIALISMS AND ACRONYMS

ASNI: American National Standards Institute

API: Application programming interface

CAT: Category (used to describe Ethernet cable type)

CPU: Central processing unit

CRT: Cathode ray tube

CSS: Cascading style sheet

DCE: Data communications equipment

DHCP: Dynamic Host Configuration Protocol

DSLL Digital subscriber line

EOL End of life

FTP: File transfer protocol

HTTPS: HyperText Transfer Protocol Secure

ISP: Internet Service Provider

LAN: Local area network

Mbps: Megabits per second

MDF: Main distribution frame

POP3: Post Office Protocol, version 3

RAM: Random Access Memory

SSH: Secure shell

TCP/IP: Transmission Control Protocol/Internet Protocol

USB: Universal Serial Bus

W3C: World Wide Web Consortium

SOLUTIONS (CONTINUED)

30: APRIL FOOL'S DAY: SAILOR FLOP DAY

Deep Lovers = Developers
Magenta Project Men: Project Management
Rumply Oops = Supply Room
Mr. Tea King = Marketing
Ed Resigns = Designers
Curt the Electrician = Client Architecture

Known Tiger = Networking
Corrective Muses = Customer Service
Prospect Hut - Tech Support
Raise Cats = Staircase
Real Votes = Elevators
Retro Moss = Restrooms

Attention all **teammates**:

Drop by the **break room** for cookies and cake as we congratulate those receiving **promotions**. We look forward to starting the next **fiscal year** together, working as **teammates**.

Happy **April Fool's Day**,
The **Executives**

31: BUZZ WORD BUZZ KILL: WORD SEARCH

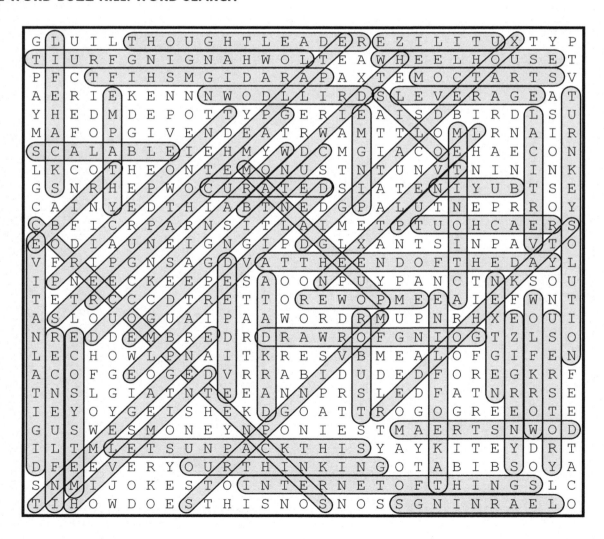

ABOUT THE ARTIST AND CREATOR

E.B. NESSER is the pen name for BETH ANDRESEN. Nesser worked in libraries for many years until one day, her job was reorganized into an IT department. She subsequently created this book.

Nesser enjoys using Firefox, taking long walks on the beach, and riding passenger trains.

She has never cooked fish in the breakroom microwave.

OTHER TITLES BY E.B. NESSER

Color and Activity Book for Librarians (Or Anybody Who Has Worked at a Library)
Victorian Fashions Worn by Cats and Dogs

Made in the USA
Middletown, DE
09 April 2020